Introduction

And we, who with unveiled faces all reflect the Lord's glory, are being transformed into His likeness with ever-increasing glory, which comes from the Lord, who is the Spirit.
2 Corinthians 3:18

Being confident of this, that He who began a good work in you will carry it on to completion until the day of Christ Jesus.
Philippians 1:6

Him we proclaim, warning everyone and teaching everyone with all wisdom, that we may present everyone mature in Christ
Colossians 1:28

Do you see a theme in these verses? Do you see what God wants to do in your life, even now? He wants to see you conformed to the image of Christ, to become complete, mature!

That is why we come together in our small groups to GROW - because we want to help each other grow into full maturity. Open up your life to others. Permit others to speak into your life. See how the Lord uses it to mature you, to grow you up.

Getting Started

What does it mean to honor someone?

Verse To Study:
But grow in the grace and knowledge of our Lord and Savior Jesus Christ. To Him be glory both now and forever! 2 Peter 3:18

To receive someone means to welcome and honor them even to the point of putting yourself aside to help them become successful and meet their desires and goals. Describe how the following women received (honored) people in these passages:

Verse To Study:
Genesis 24:15-21   1 Samuel 1:1-17   1 Samuel 25:2-31
1 Kings 17:1-16   Luke 7:36-39

_____
_____
_____
_____
_____
_____
_____
_____
_____
_____
_____
_____

_____
_____
_____
_____
_____
_____

Each woman received something when she received these people. What did each receive?

_____
_____
_____
_____

What does John 1:12 say you receive when you receive (honor) Jesus Christ?

_____
_____
_____
_____
_____
_____

Question for Week #1

Have you made the conscious decision to honor Jesus and ask Christ into your life to forgive your sins and live your life trusting Him?

What happens when people "believe" but don't welcome or honor Jesus?

_____

_____

Verses To Study:
Romans 5:8   John 1:12   John 2:23-25

Describe when you placed your trust in Christ and received Him. If you have not made this decision, what keeps you from doing so now?

_____

_____

_____

_____

Verses To Study:
Colossians 2:6-7   1 Corinthians 9:24-25   1 John 2:6

How do these verses describe your desire to grow in Christ?

_____

_____

If you don't desire to grow, what needs to change?

_____

_____

How have you made pursuing your personal relationship with the Lord a priority? Be specific.

_____
_____
_____

If you could do one thing that would improve your relationship with Jesus Christ, what do you think that would be?

_____
_____
_____

What do you think Jesus would say to do?

_____
_____
_____
_____

Do you want to learn more about what it means to grow or how to do this? Who will you learn with? (hint: this is mainly your small group)

_____
_____
_____
_____
_____

Question for Week #2

What does it mean to regularly spend time with the Lord?

What do you understand that it means to regularly spend time with someone?

_____
_____
_____
_____
_____

Verses To Study:
Psalm 119:11   Psalm 119:105

Compare how you can spend time with someone to how you can spend time with the Lord in His Word?

_____
_____
_____
_____

Read Luke 10:38-42 and describe what went on here. What does Jesus say is the one thing which is necessary?

_____
_____
_____
_____

When there is so much to do, why is this the one thing necessary?

_____
_____
_____
_____

If you have tasted the kindness of the Lord and want to grow in respect to your salvation, according to 1 Peter 2:1-3, what are you to do?

_____
_____
_____

How will you adjust your thinking so that you can take this approach to the Scriptures?

_____
_____
_____
_____

What is your plan not only to read the Bible, but also to hide it in your heart?

_____
_____
_____
_____
_____

How would you describe your prayer life?

_____

_____

_____

Verses To Study:
Colossians 4:2　　　　　　　*Matthew 14:23*
I Thessalonians 5:16-18　　*Mark 11:22-26*

What prayers in the Bible and passages about prayer grab your attention and why?

_____

_____

_____

_____

_____

_____

_____

Where would you say that you are in the battle for contentment?

_____

_____

_____

_____

Do you inwardly grumble that you don't have what others have or do you worship the Lord? Worshiping the Lord will be evidenced by a heart of thanksgiving and praise that even celebrates other people who have what you wish that you had. Please evaluate yourself.

_____
_____
_____
_____
_____

Verses To Study:
Psalm 100   Psalm 63:2-4   Hebrews 13:4-5

How would you describe your private worship with the Lord?

_____
_____
_____
_____
_____

What steps will you take to improve your devotional "quiet time"?

_____
_____
_____
_____
_____
_____

Question for Week #3

How are you trying to keep your "thought life captive"?

What does it mean to you to take your thoughts captive?

_____

_____

_____

How are you currently trying to keep your "thought life captive"?

_____

_____

Verses To Study:
2 Corinthians 10:5   Colossians 3:1-3
*Philippians 4:4-8   * Consider memorizing Philippians 4:8*

What do you think about the most as you go about your day?

_____

_____

_____

Which of these is your mind usually meditating on: worries, anxieties, fears, other people, gossip, complaints, guys, sex, material things, money, your wants, and your needs. What other negative things does your mind meditate on?

_____

_____

These thoughts may sometimes come to mind, but God calls us to a higher standard. He instructs us not to think this way.

Verses To Study:
Psalm 119:11
Isaiah 26:3 (If possible, read this verse in NIV, NLT and AMP.)

From these verses, what are some practical ways to practice keeping your thoughts captive?

_____
_____
_____
_____
_____
_____
_____

Discuss in your group some other practical ways to practice keeping your thoughts captive.

_____
_____
_____
_____
_____
_____
_____
_____

Question for Week #4

How will you strive to keep your conversations God-glorifying?

Verses To Study:
1 Timothy 4:12   *Proverbs 25:11*

Instead of thinking about things that pull you down or cause you to neglect the Holy Spirit within you, you have a higher calling.

Meditate on specific Scripture. Think of ways to initiate and serve people in your church fellowship. Contemplate ways you can honor people - even giving double honor to your pastors. Consider God's heart for those who do not know Jesus Christ.

Meditate on how you can communicate with the lost and connect them with your church fellowship. Think about the things for which you can be thankful - even your trials and difficulties. Think about Jesus' return and what heaven will be like.

With whom are you sharing the things that God is teaching you?

_____

_____

_____

Is at least one of these people older and wiser than you in the Lord? If not, with whom else fitting that description could you share on a regular basis?

_____

_____

_____

_____

Verses To Study:
Proverbs 11:13   Philippians 2:14-16a   Ephesians 4:29

What is gossip?

_____

_____

Ask yourself, "Have I been gossiping?" (Explain briefly without names or details.)

_____

_____

Ask yourself, "Have I been grumbling or complaining?" (Explain briefly without names or details.)

_____

_____

Verses To Study:
Colossians 4:6   James 1:19

How good of a listener are you? What can you do to listen even better?

_____

_____

Verses To Study:
Proverbs 24:26   Proverbs 16:10   1 Timothy 3:11

Would others describe you as honest or "double tongued" (meaning that you say one thing in one circumstance and something else in another circumstance)? Please explain.

_____

_____

Put it into Practice . .
Take a few minutes in your small group to practice what you just learned. First, spend time together talking with the Lord about the following topics. Then, discuss with your small group members any related thoughts for which you feel God may want you to follow up. (If journaling your thoughts and prayers helps you, you can use the space provided below.)

- Think about the things for which you can be thankful - even your trials and difficulties.
- Meditate on specific Scripture.
- Contemplate ways you can honor people - even giving double honor to your pastors.
- Think of ways to initiate and serve people in your church fellowship.
- Consider God's heart for those who do not know Jesus Christ.
- Meditate on how you can communicate with the lost and connect them with your church fellowship.
- Think about Jesus' return and what heaven will be like.

Journal Space

_____

_____

_____

_____

_____

_____

_____

Question for Week #5

How will you genuinely care for others?

What does care mean to you?

_____

_____

How have you been genuinely caring for others?

_____

_____

_____

Who are the key people in your life who you want to be successful?

_____

_____

_____

How have you celebrated these key people lately?

_____

_____

_____

How generous have you been with them recently?

_____

_____

_____

Verses To Study:
John 15:17   2 Corinthians 5: 14-16   Romans 15:5

Romans 12:9-13   Mark 9:35

How are you developing Christ's love for others?

_____

_____

_____

Verses To Study:
Proverbs 11:16a

How have you been a "kindhearted woman" this week? What, if anything, would you like to change for this next week?

_____

_____

_____

Verses To Study:
Matthew 28:18-20   Philemon 1:6

How would you describe your eagerness and willingness to share Christ with others so that they can know Him too? What, if anything, would you like to change for this next week?

_____

_____

_____

_____

_____

Question for Week #6

Are you a willing servant?

What does it mean to be a servant of Christ?

_____

_____

Are you willing to take on the mindset of a servant toward God and your fellow believers? Why or why not?

_____

_____

_____

Verses To Study:

Genesis 24:15-21   *Ruth 2:2-7,17-18*   *Matthew 23:11,12*

Luke 8:3   *Ephesians 6:7*   *Philippians 2:3-8*

Consider the examples above of people with a servant's heart. Honestly evaluate yourself compared to these women and to Jesus.

_____

_____

_____

Do you step up to serve when you see an opportunity? What are opportunities you have taken in the last few weeks? What are opportunities which you can take in the near future?

_____

_____

_____

_____

Do you serve cheerfully? How have you recently demonstrated (or not demonstrated) cheer in your service?

_____
_____
_____

Do you do what is required "and then some"? Please give examples.

_____
_____
_____

Opportunities can come up everywhere!
- your dorm or apartment
- your class or at work
- your family and friends
- your home group, church, or small group
- out and around town

What is the difference between serving and having a servant's heart?

_____
_____
_____
_____

How are you transitioning from serving to having a servant's heart?

_____
_____
_____

Question for Week #7

Do you know your priorities?

Verses To Study:
Matthew 6:33

*Proverbs 29:18 ***

  **If possible, read this verse from the AMP translation.*

When you look at Jesus, what priorities did he pass on to his disciples?

_____

_____

_____

When you look at your schedule, spending habits and specifically your close friends, what would you say are your priorities?

_____

_____

_____

_____

Would the person who is discipling you agree? (If you do not know who this is, assume it is your small group leader.) What, if anything, do you think they would change about your answer?

_____

_____

_____

What do you want your priorities to be?

_____

_____

_____

What would it look like if you lived by these new priorities?

_____

_____

_____

Verses To Study:
James 1:5   Proverbs 1:7

Knowing your priorities helps you know how to spend your time and how to make decisions. If you are unsure of a priority or need to make a decision, how do you seek the Lord's direction?

_____

_____

_____

_____

How open are you to seeking advice? How do you ask for input into your life?

_____

_____

_____

Can you take good advice and apply it? Please give examples.

_____
_____
_____
_____

Would your parents and the person who is discipling you agree? What, if anything, do you think they would change about your answer?

_____
_____
_____
_____

Verses To Study:
Proverbs 12:15   Proverbs 20:25

How do you filter advice from the many sources offering it?

_____
_____
_____

How can you more effectively identify and follow the good advice and filter the bad advice?

_____
_____
_____

Journal Space
You may use this space to journal additional thoughts, prayer requests, answers to prayer, etc.

Question for Week #8

How are you disciplined in your personal habits?

Verses To Study:
I Corinthians 13:11   Titus 2:11-13
Galatians 5:22-25   Luke 2:52

Do you have a good balance in your activities and daily habits? Please list out how you spend time during a typical day or week. Be sure to note time spent online, watching TV or movies, pursuing entertainment, studying or working, hanging out with various groups of friends, at church activities, in devotional times, sleeping, etc.

How are you watching over your health, eating, sleeping and exercise, in a balanced way? What goals would you like to make?

_____

_____

_____

_____

_____

_____

How are you responsible with finances? What goals would you like to make? How well do you keep a budget?

_____

_____

_____

_____

How reliable are you? How responsible are you? Please explain.

_____

_____

_____

Would you say that you show up before events start, just as they are starting, after they start or "I forgot something was going on tonight"?

_____

_____

_____

Verses To Study:
Psalm 101:2-3

What do you practice in private that you wish every Christian did?

_____
_____
_____

What private habits do you or those you live with see in your life that may compromise your conscience?

_____
_____
_____
_____

What would the person discipling you say about your personal disciplines?

_____
_____
_____
_____

What would your parents say?

_____
_____
_____
_____

Verses To Study:
Ephesians 5:15   I Timothy 4:8   Luke 16:10
I Corinthians 6:19-20   Proverbs 6:6-9

What additional goals would you like to set in light of these verses? What habits, patterns, attitudes and actions do you think the Lord wants to help you change?

_____

_____

_____

_____

_____

_____

_____

_____

Journal Space
You may use this space to journal additional thoughts, prayer requests, answers to prayer, etc.

_____

_____

_____

_____

_____

_____

_____

Question for Week #9

How are you allowing the Lord into your life concerning your behavior with guys?

Above all else, guard your heart, for it is the wellspring of life.
- Proverbs 4:23

What does it mean to you to guard your heart?

_____

_____

What does it mean to you to guard your brothers' hearts?

_____

_____

Verses To Study:
Proverbs 17:24   2 Corinthians 10:5   1 Timothy 2:9-10

How are you able to manage your thoughts about guys? Please explain without using names and specific details. (Specific names may be more appropriate for private conversations with your small group leader or the person who is discipling you.)

_____

_____

How would you describe your discretion in your interactions with guys? What are some steps which you feel the Lord may want you to take in order to show better discretion?

_____

_____

Would your words or actions be considered inappropriate, flirtatious, misleading, or not glorifying to God? Please describe briefly without names or details.

Are you humble enough talk to a friend about your behavior around guys so they can help you get an accurate view of your actions? Which friends will you do this with?

Are relationships and guys a separate part of your life that you don't want God to be a part of? Or, do you want the Lord to clearly lead here? In what ways do you need help?

Describe briefly where you stand on dating and relationships. For instance, what are you looking for in a Godly man? What is a Biblical approach to relationships? Answers to questions like these will allow you to respond appropriately when guys pursue you.

_____

_____

_____

Verses To Study:
John 4:4-26   Proverbs 11:22

If you are in a relationship, is the Lord head of this relationship? If so, please explain how the Lord is the head of this relationship.

_____

_____

_____

Have you thought about if this relationship has a future? Where is this relationship going?

_____

_____

Do you have Biblical standards for your relationship? If so, what are they?

_____

_____

_____

Verses To Study:
Proverbs 18:15   Ephesians 5:3   1Timothy 5:1-2
1 Corinthians 7:1 (NAS) 2 Timothy 2:22   1 Timothy 5:21
Ephesians 5:15-18   Matthew 28:19-20

What do the verses above describe as personal standards that should be in place for a relationship?

_____

_____

_____

_____

Verses To Study:
I Corinthians 6:18-20   1 Thessalonians 4:3-8

Why is it important when the Bible says, "flee all sexual immorality"?

_____

_____

Verses To Study:
John 8:1-11   Acts 3:19   2 Corinthians 6:9-11

You can be forgiven of any past action, even sexual immorality. What do you understand needs to be done to experience forgiveness and restoration?

_____

_____

_____

Verses To Study:
1 John 1:7-9   James 5:16

If needed, what steps do you need to take in order to re-establish your desire to glorify and honor God, especially with your body?

_____

_____

_____

_____

Thinking ahead to your future, what have you read that the Bible says about being a wife?

_____

_____

_____

_____

What have you read that the Bible says about your husband's role?

_____

_____

_____

_____

What have you read that the Bible says about children?

_____

_____

_____

Journal Space

You may use this space to journal additional thoughts, prayer requests, answers to prayer, etc.

Question for Week #10

How are you trusting the Lord with your future?

Verses To Study:
Jeremiah 29:11   Proverbs 3:5,6   John 10:10
Hebrews 11:1   2 Peter 1:3

How are you growing in that faith that God will come through for you?

_____

_____

_____

_____

Verses To Study:
Ephesians 3:16-19   Jeremiah 31:3   Isaiah 55:10-12

How have you tried to give your hopes for your future husband, future career, family, friends, and finances to God?

_____

_____

_____

_____

This is not a one-time prayer for most women, but rather a continual prayer to seek the Lord and to trust Him for these areas.

Verses To Study:
*Psalm 25:3a**   *Psalm 71:14*   *Micah 7:7*
Romans 4:18-22 *Romans 15:13*

How will you strive to be content in the here and now?

_____
_____
_____
_____
_____
_____
_____
_____
_____
_____
_____

I am not saying this because I am in need, for I have learned to be content whatever the circumstances. I know what it is to be in need, and I know what it is to have plenty. I have learned the secret of being content in any and every situation, whether well fed or hungry, whether living in plenty or in want. I can do everything through him who gives me strength.
- Philippians 4:11-13

Journal Space
You may use this space to journal additional thoughts, prayer requests, answers to prayer, etc.

Journal Space

You may use this space to journal additional thoughts, prayer requests, answers to prayer, etc.

New Goals & Disciplines

As you complete this study, you may use the following space to set goals and establish new disciplines in your life. Take them one or two at a time and check them off as you complete them or integrate them into your regular routine.

○ _____

○ _____

○ _____

○ _____

○ _____

○ _____

○ _____

○ _____

*But the noble man makes noble plans,
and by noble deeds he stands.
Isaiah 32:8*